The First Flight

Written by Mary-Anne Creasy

Flying Start
to Literacy®

Contents

Introduction

For thousands of years people had wanted to fly, but no one had been able to.

When the hot-air balloon was invented in France over 220 years ago, people were finally able to fly.

This is the story of the first flight.

Chapter 1

Ideas and experiments

Over 220 years ago, two brothers
had an idea while they were watching
a fire in their fireplace. They watched
the smoke and sparks rising from
the fire.

The brothers wondered if hot smoke
could be used in a flying machine
that could carry people in the air.

The brothers did some experiments.

They made a frame from very light
wood and covered it with a silk bag.
They lit a fire under the opening
of the bag. The bag floated up.
This was the first hot-air balloon.

The brothers thought that the burning and the smoke created a special gas that made the balloon rise.

But they were wrong. The balloon rose because it was filled with hot air, and hot air rises.

The brothers decided to build a bigger balloon. The brothers lit a fire under the balloon.

The balloon went up so fast and pulled so hard that it broke the rope that tied it to the ground.

The balloon floated more than two kilometres away.

Chapter 2

Showing the public

The brothers were so excited with
their invention that they decided
to show it to the public. They built
a huge balloon made of cloth pieces.
The cloth pieces were held together
with nearly two thousand buttons.

This balloon rose more than
one kilometre into the air and
travelled a distance of two kilometres.

People were amazed.

The brothers wanted to show their wonderful flying machine to the King and Queen of France.

The brothers planned to have people riding in the balloon. But the King would not allow people to fly in the balloon because no one knew if the air high in the sky was safe to breathe.

King of France,
Louis XVI

Queen of France,
Marie Antoinette

So the brothers decided that a sheep,
a duck and a rooster would ride in the
balloon instead.

The brothers made a huge fire. They burned straw, wool and even hundreds of old shoes to make the fire in the balloon very smoky.

The balloon went up high in the sky. The animals travelled up more than one kilometre into the air and landed safely nearly three kilometres away.

The sheep, the duck and the rooster were the first living things to fly in a hot-air balloon.

Chapter 3
Any volunteers?

The brothers were very pleased with their hot-air balloon, but they wanted to show that people could fly in it.

They did a test with two passengers in the balloon. To make sure that the people were safe, they tied ropes from the balloon to the ground. The test was a success. The balloon lifted up into the air.

After the test, the brothers decided it was time to let passengers travel in the hot-air balloon.

Chapter 4
People can fly

The brothers built a large balloon
to carry passengers. This balloon
was more than 20 metres high.

This would be the first time that people
would travel from one place to another
in a hot-air balloon.

At first everything went well. The
balloon rose into the air for about
one kilometre and flew gently
over the city.

But then the cloth of the balloon started to burn.

One of the people in the hot-air balloon knew that the whole balloon could soon catch fire and fall. So he took off his coat and used it to beat out the fire.

Slowly the balloon sank to the ground, landing about 12 kilometres from where it had started. No one was hurt.

The first flight was a success.

Today people still fly in hot-air balloons. Modern balloons look very different and they are much safer.